7/16

EDGE
BOOKS

VS
BUG WARS

TARANTULA VS. TARANTULA HAWK

BY LINDSY O'BRIEN

CLASH OF THE GIANTS

CONSULTANT:
Christiane Weirauch
Professor of Entomology,
Department of Entomology
University of California, Riverside

CAPSTONE PRESS
a capstone imprint

Edge Books are published by Capstone Press,
1710 Roe Crest Drive, North Mankato, Minnesota 56003
www.mycapstone.com

Library of Congress Cataloging-in-Publication Data
O'Brien, Lindsy, author.
Tarantula vs. tarantula hawk : clash of the giants / by Lindsy O'Brien.
pages cm.—(Edge books. Bug wars)
Audience: Ages 9–10.
Audience: Grades 4 to 6.
Summary: "Describes the characteristics of tarantulas and tarantula hawks, and what may
happen when these bugs encounter one another in nature"—Provided
by publisher.
ISBN 978-1-4914-8064-9 (library binding)
ISBN 978-1-4914-8068-7 (paperback)
ISBN 978-1-4914-8072-4 (eBook PDF)
1. Tarantulas—Juvenile literature. 2. Tarantulas—Predators of—Juvenile literature.
3. Pepsis—Juvenile literature. 4. Spider wasps—Behavior—Juvenile literature. I. Title.
QL458.42.T5O27 2016
595.4'4—dc23   2015024334

Editorial Credits
Aaron Sautter, editor; Russell Griesmer, designer; Jo Miller, media researcher;
Katy LaVigne, production specialist

Photo Credits
Alamy: Bob Jensen, 11, (bottom); Dreamstime: Sb Sullivan, 7, (top); Glow Images:
ImageBroker RM/Dirk Funhoff, Cover (left), 4, 9 (top); National Geographic Creative:
John Cancalosi, 7 (bottom), 21; Newscom: Custom Medical Stock Photo/Educational
Images LTD, 15 (bottom), 22, Custom Medical Stock Photo/John Reid, 13 (top),
ImageBROKER/Thomas Vinke, 11 (top), Minden Pictures/Mark Moffett, 25, 27,
Photoshot/NHPA/James Carmichael, 15 (top), Reuters/Henry Romero, 13 (bottom),
Universal Images Group/Dorling Kindersley, 17; Science Source: Kenneth M. Highfill,
23; Shutterstock: Agustin Esmoris, Cover (right and back), 5, 9 (bottom), 20; SuperStock:
Exactostock-1598/Robert Oelman, 29; Wikimedia: Astrobradley, 19

Design Elements
Capstone and Shutterstock

Printed and bound in US.
007521CGS16

TABLE OF CONTENTS

WELCOME TO BUG WARS!

Whether you see them or not, bug wars are raging around you every day. **Predators** and **prey** fight one another for survival. Bugs fight for places to live, to **reproduce**, and to protect their young. Bug battles are often intense. Keep your eyes peeled and you may just see a bug war happening near you!

predator—an animal that hunts other animals for food

prey—an animal hunted by another animal for food

reproduce—to breed and have offspring

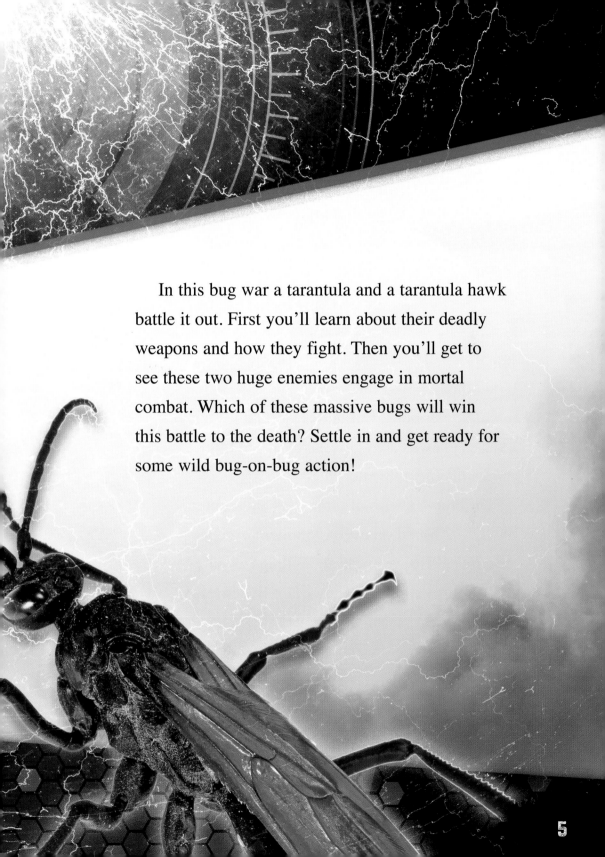

In this bug war a tarantula and a tarantula hawk battle it out. First you'll learn about their deadly weapons and how they fight. Then you'll get to see these two huge enemies engage in mortal combat. Which of these massive bugs will win this battle to the death? Settle in and get ready for some wild bug-on-bug action!

THE COMBATANTS

Many people fear tarantulas and tarantula hawks. That's not surprising. Both bugs are big and look scary. Tarantulas are huge, hairy spiders with big fangs. Tarantula hawks are giant wasps with nasty stingers. Tarantula hawks belong to a group of wasps that hunt spiders—especially tarantulas. Both of these huge bugs are fierce toward other bugs. But neither tarantulas nor tarantula hawks are aggressive toward humans unless they feel threatened.

Different **species** of tarantulas and tarantula hawks are found on every continent except Antarctica. However, these big bugs usually prefer warm climates. They often live in deserts and rainforests around the world.

species—a group of plants or animals that share common characteristics

SIZE AND WEIGHT

Tarantulas are huge spiders. Most have leg spans of about 5 inches (13 centimeters). That's about as big as an adult's hand. However, the Goliath bird-eating tarantula can grow up to 1 foot (30.5 cm) long! Although tarantulas are large, they aren't very heavy. Most weigh only 1 to 3 ounces (28 to 85 grams).

Tarantula hawks are smaller than tarantulas—but they're still one of the world's biggest insects. North American tarantula hawks can have 3-inch (7.6-cm) wingspans. The largest tarantula hawks live in the rainforests of South America. These wasps can have wingspans up to 4.5 inches (11.6 cm) wide. In flight, these huge insects may look like small birds.

FIERCE FACT

THE TARANTULA HAWK WAS VOTED THE STATE INSECT OF NEW MEXICO IN 1989.

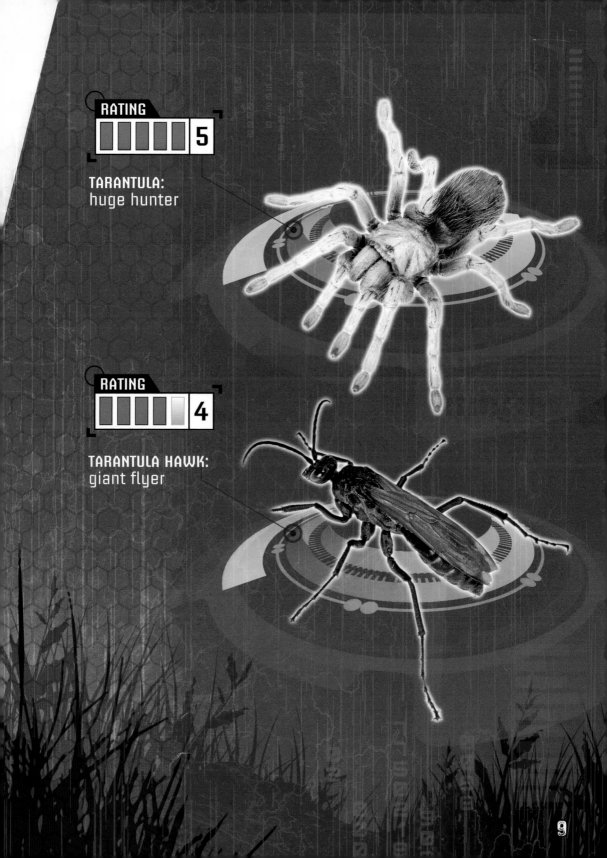

RATING 5

TARANTULA:
huge hunter

RATING 4

TARANTULA HAWK:
giant flyer

MOVEMENT AND STRENGTH

Tarantulas have two or three retractable claws at the end of their legs. When not in use these claws can be pulled in like a cat's claws. The claws help the big spiders climb on steep or slippery surfaces. Tarantulas usually move slowly and carefully. Sometimes they might sit so still that they appear to be dead. But when hunting, they are able to lunge quickly at prey.

Tarantula hawks make short flights by beating their wings rapidly. They can also be found scampering quickly across the desert sand. These big wasps use both movements as they search for prey.

Tarantula hawks are also very strong. They can drag much larger tarantulas across the ground. Sometimes they can even fly awkwardly with tarantulas gripped in their legs.

RATING

3

TARANTULA:
strong, but
slow stalker

RATING

5

TARANTULA HAWK:
quick and strong flier

retractable—able to be pulled back from
an extended position

DEFENSES

When it comes to defense, the tarantula is very creative. The spider usually hides inside its burrow. It often hides the entrance by covering it with plants or dirt. The tarantula may also spin a line of silk outside the burrow entrance. This silk acts like a tripwire that alerts the spider when prey or enemies get close.

When threatened, the tarantula raises its front legs above its head. People often mistake this as a sign that the tarantula is about to attack. However, this action is meant more as a warning. By making itself look larger, the tarantula hopes that enemies will leave it alone.

Tarantula hawk defenses involve the use of color and smell. These wasps have bright red wings and metallic blue-black bodies. These bright colors act as a warning and a sign of danger to other animals. The wasps also give off a smell that warns predators about their powerful venom.

burrow—a hole in the ground made or used by an animal
venom—poisonous liquid produced by some animals

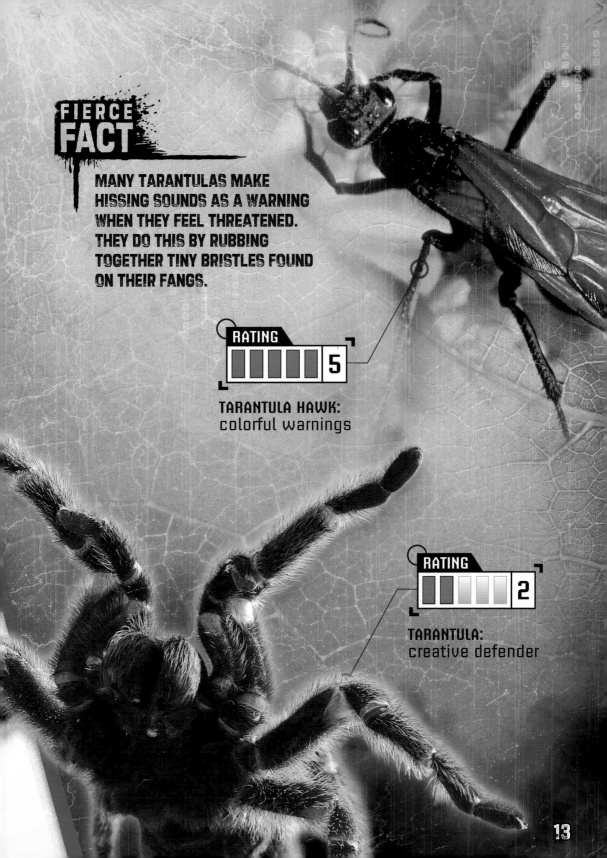

MANY TARANTULAS MAKE
HISSING SOUNDS AS A WARNING
WHEN THEY FEEL THREATENED.
THEY DO THIS BY RUBBING
TOGETHER TINY BRISTLES FOUND
ON THEIR FANGS.

RATING 5

TARANTULA HAWK:
colorful warnings

RATING 2

TARANTULA:
creative defender

WEAPONS

A tarantula's main weapons are its strength, big fangs, and venom. However, tarantula venom is weaker than most types of bee venom. It's only strong enough to **paralyze** insects and a few small animals. But tarantulas may just crush their prey with their very strong jaws.

Tarantulas are also equipped with special **urticating** bristles on their abdomens. When they're threatened, the spiders can flick these barbed hairs at enemies to chase them away.

The tarantula hawk's primary weapons are its large stinger and deadly venom. A female's stinger can measure up to 0.33 inch (0.8 cm) long. Its venom can paralyze victims in a matter of seconds. The tarantula hawk can also use its strong legs and hooked claws to grapple with its prey. The ability to fly also gives the tarantula hawk a big advantage during a fight.

> **paralyze**—to cause the loss of the ability to control the muscles
>
> **urticate**—to cause painful itching or irritation

5

TARANTULA:
big poisonous fangs,
strong jaws

FIERCE FACT

ACCORDING TO THE SCHMIDT STING PAIN INDEX, TARANTULA HAWKS HAVE THE SECOND MOST PAINFUL STING IN THE WORLD. THEIR VENOM ISN'T DEADLY TO HUMANS. BUT IT'S POWERFUL ENOUGH TO CAUSE AN ADULT TO FALL TO THE GROUND SCREAMING IN PAIN.

RATING

3

TARANTULA HAWK:
large stinger,
hooked claws

TARANTULA ATTACK STYLE

The tarantula is a sneaky and patient hunter. It normally hides in its burrow and waits for prey to pass by. The spider then lunges from the burrow entrance to ambush its prey. Once outside the tarantula grabs its victim with its strong legs and holds it down. The spider holds its prey long enough to inject venom with its fangs. After the prey is dead, the spider's fangs produce digestive **enzymes** that liquefy the victim's insides. The tarantula can then suck up the soupy meal through its strawlike mouthparts.

FIERCE FACT

TARANTULAS USUALLY EAT INSECTS SUCH AS CRICKETS, GRASSHOPPERS, AND BEETLES. BUT THEY ARE ALSO KNOWN TO EAT MICE, LIZARDS, AND FROGS.

TARANTULA:
patient ambusher

enzyme—a protein that helps break down food

TARANTULA HAWK ATTACK STYLE

Tarantula hawks use their sense of smell to hunt for and find tarantula burrows. When attacking, some tarantula hawks just sting their prey wherever they can. But the big wasps will often try to push tarantulas over to sting them on their soft stomachs.

Once stung the tarantula becomes paralyzed. The tarantula hawk sometimes drags its victim back to its burrow. This can be more than 300 feet (91 meters) away. But the wasp will often use the spider's own burrow instead. The wasp then lays one egg on the tarantula. After the egg hatches, the larva starts to eat the tarantula alive. The tarantula won't die until the larva eats an important organ. The larva avoids doing this to keep the tarantula alive as long as possible. The whole process can take up to 32 days.

FIERCE FACT

ADULT TARANTULA HAWKS DON'T ACTUALLY EAT SPIDERS. THEY USUALLY DRINK NECTAR FROM FLOWERS INSTEAD. HOWEVER, THEY SOMETIMES LIKE TO EAT SWEET FERMENTED FRUIT.

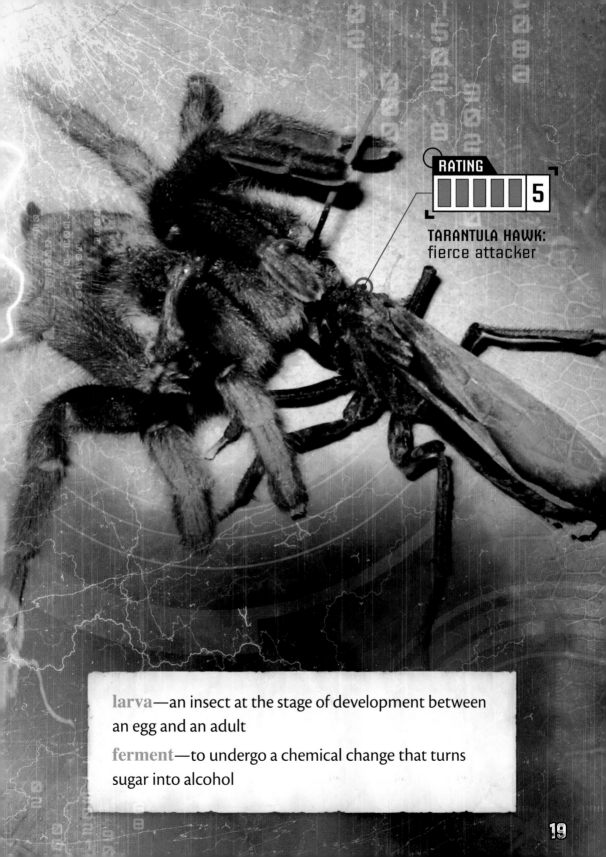

RATING
5

TARANTULA HAWK:
fierce attacker

larva—an insect at the stage of development between an egg and an adult

ferment—to undergo a chemical change that turns sugar into alcohol

GET READY TO RUMBLE!

Coming up—a bug war that's sure to be intense! The tarantula is on full alert. Will that be enough when the deadly tarantula hawk comes looking for him? The tarantula is bigger, stronger, and has dangerous fangs. But the tarantula hawk has the advantages of speed and her powerful, paralyzing venom. Less than 1 in 100 tarantulas survive in battle against tarantula hawks. Will our spider be one of the lucky ones? Get ready for an awesome bug-on-bug smackdown!

ONE LAST THING...

Tarantulas and tarantula hawks often meet and fight to the death in the wild. But the following bug war is fiction. Although this battle isn't real, actual battles just like it take place all over the world every day.

THE BATTLE BEGINS!

A tarantula sleeps in its desert burrow. His stomach is full from the crickets he ate last night. After his feast, the spider plugged his home's entrance with webbing and dead leaves. He also ran a string of silk in front of the entrance. If more tasty insects wander by, he'll know when they hit his tripwire. However, another dangerous hunter is prowling nearby.

FIERCE FACT

OTHER THAN TARANTULA HAWKS, TARANTULAS HAVE FEW NATURAL ENEMIES. ROADRUNNERS AND BULLFROGS SOMETIMES EAT TARANTULAS. SCORPIONS MAY ALSO OVERCOME TARANTULAS WITH THEIR POWERFUL VENOM AND CLAWS.

Outside, a tarantula hawk runs across the sand. The sun gleams off her shiny blue-black body and red wings. She darts and sniffs while seeking out her prey's hiding place. Suddenly she stops. She can smell the tarantula's burrow. Then she sees a glint of sunlight on a thin thread of webbing. It's the spider's tripwire. She steps up to the silk thread and taps it with her leg.

Below ground, the tarantula wakes. *Prey*, he thinks. He makes his way through the tunnel and gets into position. He pushes open the plug to peek outside. If he sees another juicy cricket, he'll lunge and pounce on it. He waits at his burrow entrance. He can almost taste his next meal.

CLOSE CALLS

But suddenly the tarantula's burrow is filled with sunlight. The tarantula hawk has ripped away the entrance plug. The tarantula is surprised and scared. He raises up his legs to warn his enemy. The big wasp backs off. She drops the plug and beats her wings to lift herself into the air.

Before she gets far, the tarantula lunges at her! But the cunning wasp is too quick. She darts just out of the spider's reach. The tarantula stands up tall with his legs raised. The tarantula hawk sees her chance. She swoops and slams into him, knocking him off balance. The big spider falls backward and lays sprawled on his back.

FIERCE FACT

TARANTULAS OFTEN LOSE LEGS IN BATTLE. BUT THEY CAN REGROW LOST LEGS WHEN THEY MOLT.

The tarantula flails his legs. He's desperate to flip back onto his feet. The tarantula hawk gets into position and dives for her prey's stomach. But the tarantula is faster. He twists hard and lands on his eight hairy legs.

The big wasp dives for the tarantula again, but he's ready this time. He leaps at her and grabs her with his legs. Tiny barbed bristles shoot from his belly and into his enemy. The wasp's wings crunch as the tarantula squeezes her body. She is caught.

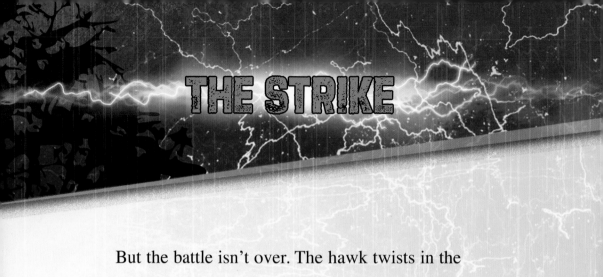

THE STRIKE

But the battle isn't over. The hawk twists in the tarantula's grip. She slashes at the spider with the hooked claw on her free leg. The tarantula's hold loosens. Suddenly the fierce hunter gives one last powerful push and beats her wings hard. The hawk finally twists out of the spider's grasp. As she breaks free, the tarantula loses its balance. Once again he falls backward to the ground—exposing his soft stomach.

The tarantula hawk doesn't wait this time. Before her prey can flip himself over, she plunges her stinger into his soft belly.

Within seconds, the tarantula freezes in place. One leg is still raised above his head. To be sure the spider can't move, the hunter stings her prey again. Then she lands a few inches away and waits. Finally she knows that the tarantula is paralyzed. She's won this fight.

The tarantula hawk then hooks the tarantula with her curved claws. She drags the spider to his own burrow. After a moment, both bugs disappear underground.

THE AFTERMATH

Deep in the dark burrow, the tarantula hawk lays one egg on the tarantula's stomach. This spider is large, so she fertilizes the egg. She then flies off in search of another tarantula to battle.

Back in the burrow, the egg hatches into a larva that looks like a white grub. It first eats a hole into the tarantula's stomach. Then it works its way into the spider's body. To keep its food source alive, it avoids eating important organs like the heart or lungs. This gives the larva a fresh store of food as it grows. When the larva does eat one of the vital organs, the spider finally dies.

When it's grown large enough, the larva forms a cocoon. Inside the cocoon it transforms into a female tarantula hawk. After it emerges, the new tarantula hawk will begin its own deadly hunt for tarantulas.

AFTER A MALE AND FEMALE TARANTULA HAWK MATE, THE FEMALE CAN LAY AN EGG. THE FEMALE CAN EITHER FERTILIZE THE EGG OR LEAVE IT UNFERTILIZED. FERTILIZED EGGS PRODUCE FEMALE WASPS WHILE MALES COME FROM UNFERTILIZED EGGS.

GLOSSARY

burrow (BUHR-oh)—a hole in the ground made or used by an animal

enzyme (EN-zime)—a protein that helps break down food

exoskeleton (ek-soh-SKE-luh-tuhn)—a structure on the outside of an animal that gives it support

ferment (fur-MENT)—to undergo a chemical change that turns sugar into alcohol

larva (LAR-vuh)—an insect at the stage of development between an egg and an adult

paralyze (PAY-ruh-lize)—to cause the loss of the ability to control the muscles

predator (PRED-uh-tur)—an animal that hunts other animals for food

prey (PRAY)—an animal hunted by another animal for food

reproduce (ree-pruh-DOOSE)—to breed and have offspring

retractable (rih-TRACT-uh-buhl)—able to be pulled back from an extended position

species (SPEE-sheez)—a group of plants or animals that share common characteristics

urticate (UR-tuh-kayt)—to cause painful itching or irritation

venom (VEN-uhm)—poisonous liquid produced by some animals

READ MORE

Meinking, Mary. *Tarantula vs. Bird. Predator vs. Prey.* Chicago: Raintree, 2011.

Murawski, Darlyne. *Ultimate Bug-Opedia.* Washington, D.C.: National Geographic, 2013.

Parker, Steve. *Bug Wars: Deadly Insects and Spiders Go Head-to-Head.* Animal Wars. New York: Ticktock Books, 2014.

INTERNET SITES

FactHound offers a safe, fun way to find Internet sites related to this book. All of the sites on FactHound have been researched by our staff

Here's all you do:

Visit *www.facthound.com*

Type in this code: 9781491480649

 **Super-cool stuff!** Check out projects, games and lots more at
www.capstonekids.com

INDEX